If a Petoskey Stone Could Talk

written by Brittany Darga
illustrated by Jennifer Franzoni

Mission Point Press

Readers are encouraged to go to www.MissionPointPress.com to contact the author, or to contact the publisher about how to buy this book in bulk at a discounted rate.

MISSION POINT PRESS

Published by Mission Point Press

2554 Chandler Rd.

Traverse City, MI 49696

(231) 421-9513

MissionPointPress.com

ISBN: 978-1-961302-44-0 (softcover)
ISBN: 978-1-961302-43-3 (hardcover)

Library of Congress Control Number: 2024904290

Printed in the United States of America

To my husband, who is my best friend, my soulmate, and my rock
Brittany Darga

For Henry and Charlie
Jennifer Franzoni

Every year when the sun is high and the air feels hot and a little sticky, we head to the shores of Lake Michigan.

Here, the teal and navy-blue colors of the water stretch farther than any rainbow can reach.

Slight waves lap against the shore, and off in the distance we can see giant hills known as sand dunes.

We grab a spot with our towels, sand buckets, shovels, snacks, and water bottles in the beach bag my mom always brings.

Swimming is on our minds, but the thousands of rocks in every shade of blue, red, orange, gray, brown, and white capture our attention first.

My dad is the first to pick up a rock.

It's gray and flat and fits perfectly in between his thumb and pointer finger.

He heads off to skip it across the water.

I count as it bounces and jumps across the smooth, clear water at least eight times.

Soon, my two sisters and I
put our heads down and look
for rocks in all different shapes
and sizes.

"Look at this little blue one,
the color of the lake," I say.

"Look at this brown one, the color
of the wet sand," my sister says,
holding up a faded, speckled rock.

"Mom, this one has dots
that look like the sun,"
my other sister says as she holds
a gray rock that fits perfectly
in her fist.

"That's a Petoskey stone,"
says my mom.

"W

hat's a Petoskey stone?" we all ask at once, each trying to be the first.

"It's a fossil," says my dad. "A fossil is an imprint left behind from a plant or animal from many, many years ago."

Trilobite

Brachiopod

Petoskey stone

"Just one single stone is millions of years old and holds so much history. A Petoskey stone is perhaps the oldest thing you'll ever hold.

"Imagine if a Petoskey stone could talk."

Horn Coral

Did you know?

A Petoskey stone is one of many fossils that can be found in Michigan. Other common fossils found on Michigan beaches include:

Horn coral

Scientifically known as Rugosa, these fossils were once horn-shaped coral.

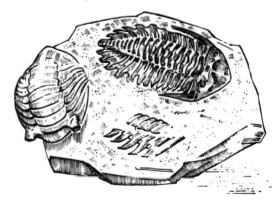

Trilobite

About the size of a penny, trilobites are from arthropods (think scorpions, centipedes, crayfish, shrimp) living millions of years ago. The animal that makes trilobites is no longer around today.

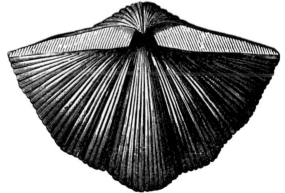

Brachiopod

These fossils were once marine animals resembling a clam or mussel. They have two shells that mirror each other. Some brachiopods are still around today.

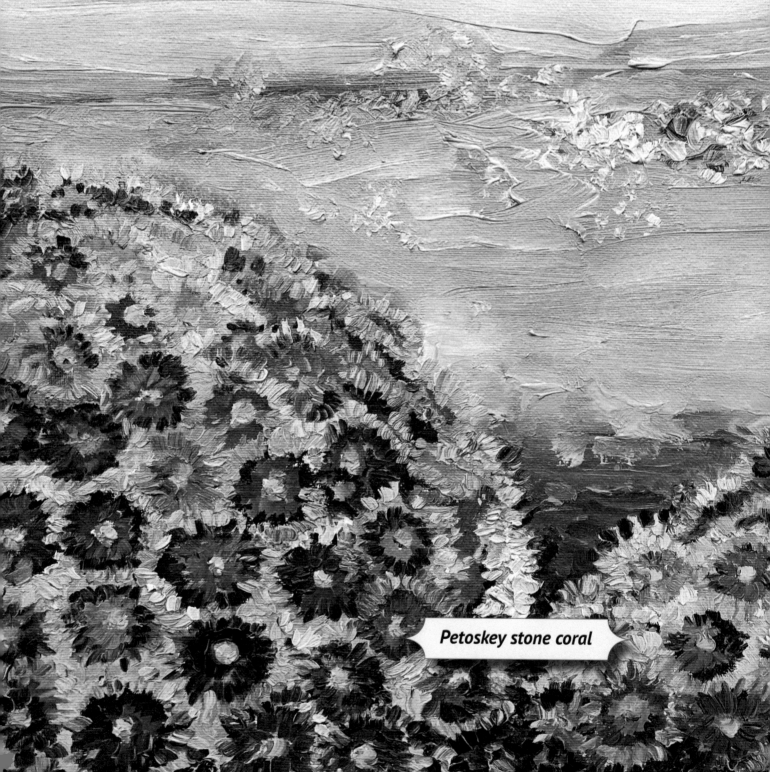

My mom grins and says, "If a Petoskey stone could talk, it might say, '**Pick me! Pick me!** I am the most special rock of all. I was once a living animal called coral.'"

"What's coral?" we all ask at once.

"Coral is a type of animal that lives in the ocean. Once upon a time, Michigan was covered by a warm, salty ocean, and one of the first animals to live in the ocean was coral. Coral might not LOOK like an animal but it is!"

Petoskey stone coral

Did you know?

Coral is a saltwater animal and no longer lives in the freshwater Great Lakes. But because there was once A LOT of this coral, there are still many, many Petoskey stones that wash up on shore from the wind and waves.

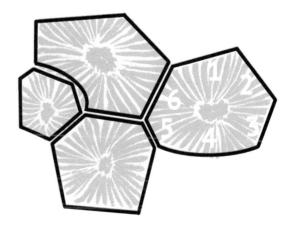

Petoskey stones are known for their repeating pattern of hexagon (6-sided shape) bursts.

The hexagon shape is called corallite, and each corallite held a single animal. The animal opened its mouth, exposing tentacles. The tentacles took in food, but they could also sting other creatures that got too close.

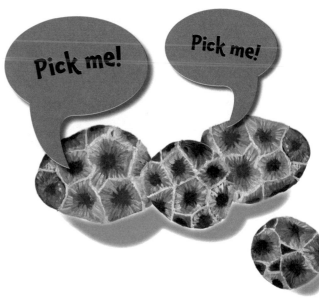

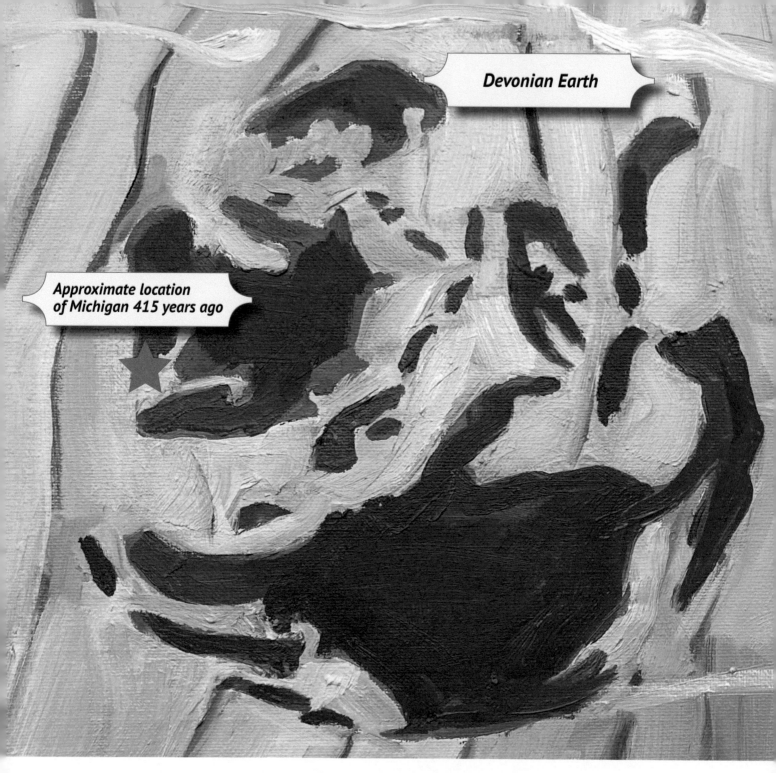

Devonian Earth

Approximate location of Michigan 415 years ago

Did you know?

Petoskey stones have been around for millions of years, before most animals and living things came to be what they are today. They were formed in the Devonian Period, which is part of the Paleozoic Era.

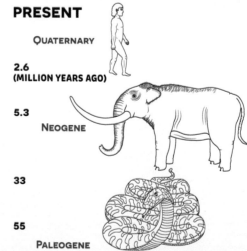

PRESENT

Quaternary

2.6
(MILLION YEARS AGO)

5.3
Neogene

33

55

Paleogene

CENOZOIC ERA

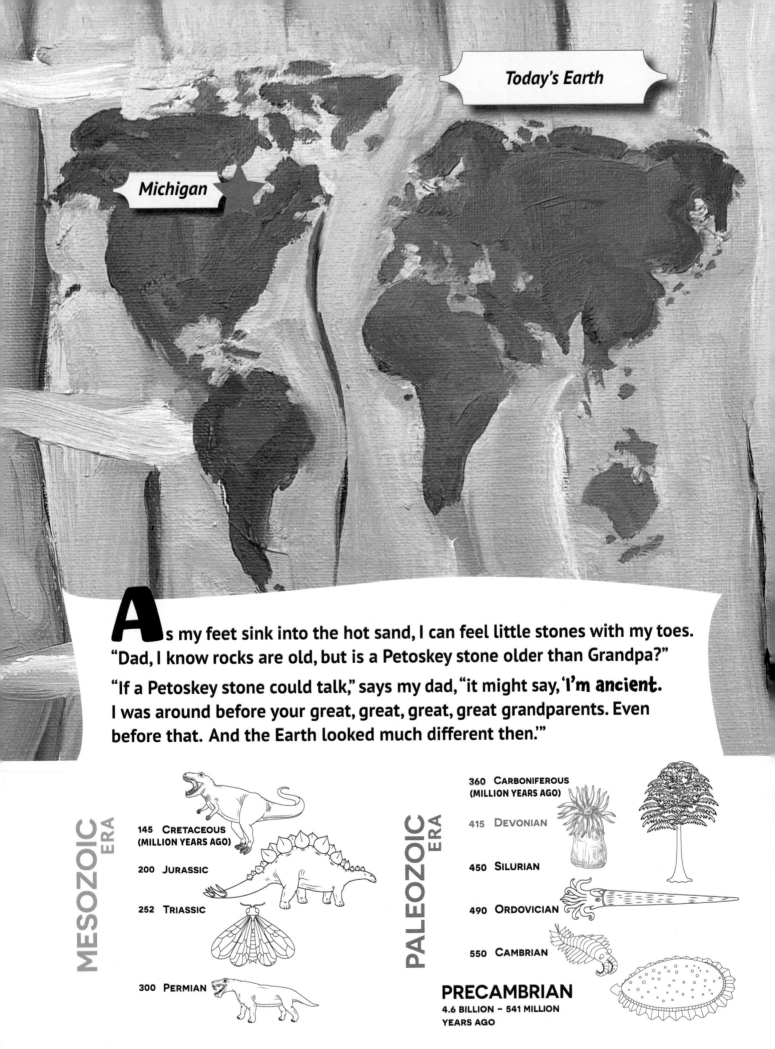

Today's Earth

Michigan

As my feet sink into the hot sand, I can feel little stones with my toes. "Dad, I know rocks are old, but is a Petoskey stone older than Grandpa?"

"If a Petoskey stone could talk," says my dad, "it might say, 'I'm **ancient**. I was around before your great, great, great, great grandparents. Even before that. And the Earth looked much different then.'"

MESOZOIC ERA

145 CRETACEOUS
(MILLION YEARS AGO)

200 JURASSIC

252 TRIASSIC

300 PERMIAN

PALEOZOIC ERA

360 CARBONIFEROUS
(MILLION YEARS AGO)

415 DEVONIAN

450 SILURIAN

490 ORDOVICIAN

550 CAMBRIAN

PRECAMBRIAN
4.6 BILLION – 541 MILLION
YEARS AGO

Then my mom says, "If a Petoskey stone could talk, it might say, 'I'm wise. I was around even before the city or town you live in was built, and before the roads you drive on were created ... way, way before.' This is what the plants and animals looked like then."

Did you know?

Petoskey stones were formed in the middle of the DEVONIAN PERIOD, about 400 million years ago. This period is known as "the age of the fish" because this was when many different types of sea life first evolved on the Earth. Much of what scientists know about the Devonian Period comes from fossils like the Petoskey stone.

I step closer to the water to let the cool waves touch my feet. I try to imagine what the world was like when Petoskey stones were created. My sister walks in front of me, wrapped in her dinosaur beach towel. Then I wonder out loud, "Have Petoskey stones seen dinosaurs?"

"If a Petoskey stone could talk," my mom says, "it might say, 'I'm **brave.**'
After millions of years, the big, salty ocean dried up and animals changed. But the Petoskey stones were still here, right where you are standing. Petoskey stones are older than the dinosaurs."

"If a Petoskey stone could talk," my mom goes on, "it might say, 'I am strong. I survived through the extinction of dinosaurs.'"

My sisters hold up their arms to show how strong they are.

Did you know?

No one really knows why the dinosaurs died, or became extinct, some 65 million years ago. But scientists have ideas, such as an asteroid hitting the Earth, or gradual changes to the Earth's climate. Either way, Petoskey stones weathered the storm!

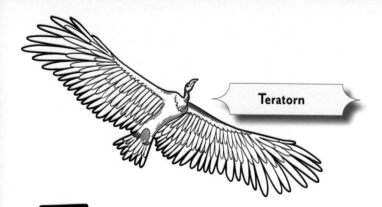

Teratorn

Then our dad tells us about the Ice Age. "Millions of years after the dinosaurs died, the Earth got very, very cold. Massive ice sheets called glaciers formed. They were taller than the tallest building! The glaciers buried the coral and everything else.

"If a Petoskey stone could talk," he says, "it might say, 'I'm **patient**. I waited and waited. I waited underneath glaciers for millions of years.'"

"Wow," I say, "that's a lot of patience. I have a hard enough time waiting for dinner!"

Smilodon

Did you know?

Over time, Michigan went from being in a warm, tropical place to being covered in ice. Michigan and many of the northern parts of the world were covered in glaciers. Big animals with thick coats of fur — animals like the woolly mammoths, mastodons, and saber-toothed tigers wandered around here.

One good thing about the Ice Age was that people could walk on the frozen water. Some of them walked from Russia to Alaska.

"I'm patient."

My dad says, "The Ice Age seemed to last forever, but finally, the Earth began to warm up. Plants and animals, like the trees and deer you have seen formed and grew.

"As the glaciers melted, they left behind Michigan's beautiful lakes and beaches ... and the ancient Petoskey stones."

Mom says, "If a Petoskey stone could talk, it might say, 'I'm **determined**. My waiting paid off. When the glaciers moved, I was uncovered and looked like beautiful rays of sunlight.'"

Did you know?

There are still glaciers today, but they're all north of us, closer to the North Pole. That's where our old glaciers went, melting and shrinking as they moved. They were so big, that as they moved, they tore up the ground, leaving big holes and cracks; those are our lakes and rivers. They also tore up the old salty bed of the long-ago coral sea, leaving pieces of fossilized coral (Petoskey stones) in all different shapes and sizes. Over time, the waves and sand have polished the Petoskey stones smooth. We know that Petoskey stones were first uncovered about 11,000 years ago. That is a VERY long time ago!

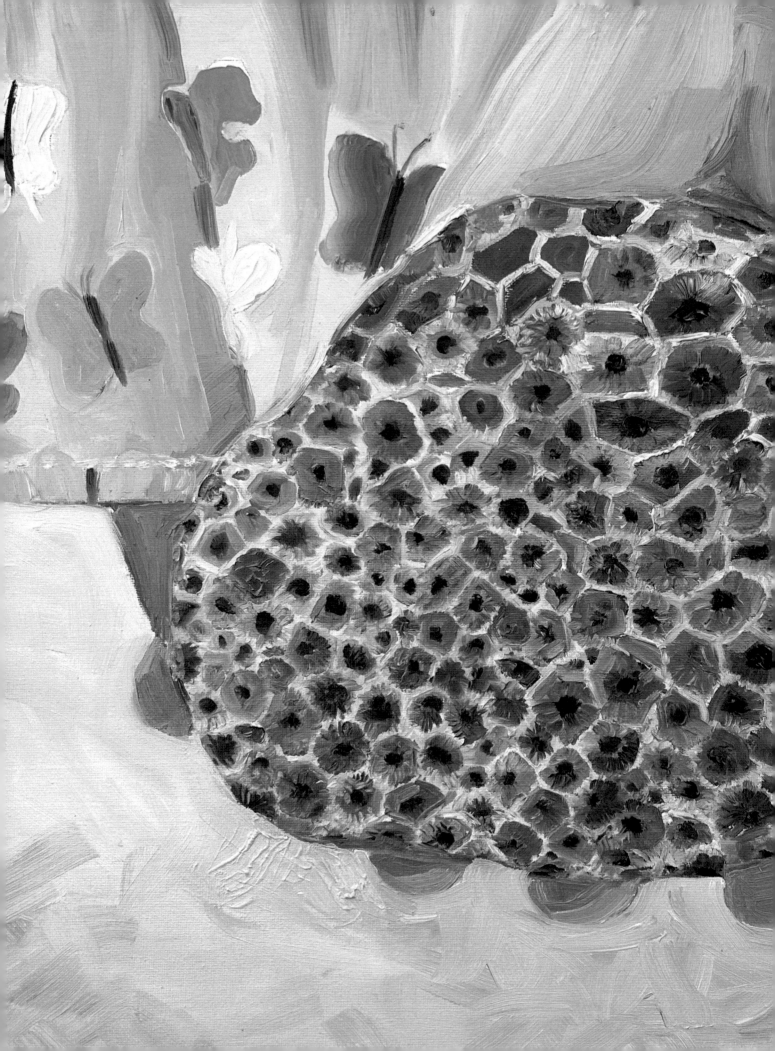

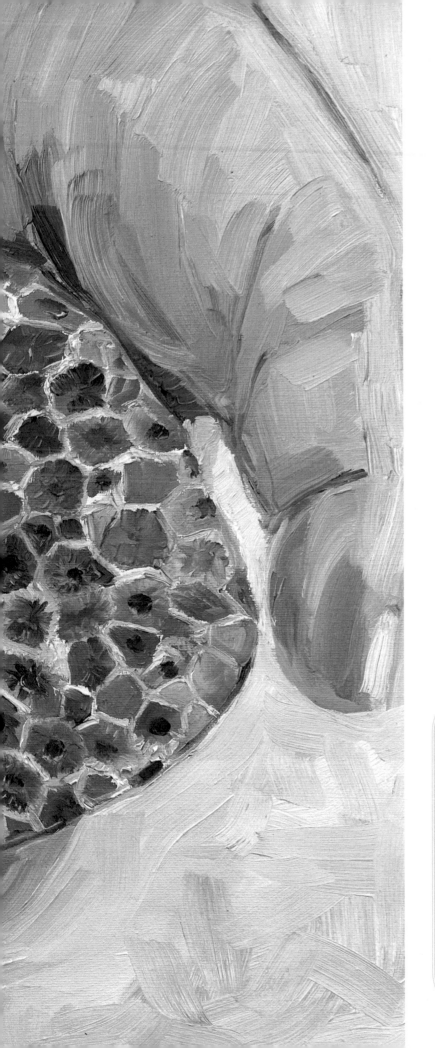

"If a Petoskey stone could talk," my dad says to us, "it might say, 'I'm **unique!** I am most commonly found on Michigan beaches.'"

"I wonder what else Petoskey stones would say?" my dad asks.

"**I'm sensitive**," I say. "My pattern can only be seen when I'm wet."

"**I'm important**," my sister says. "They seem like a big deal in Michigan."

"Yes, unique, sensitive, and important — a Petoskey stone is all of those things," says my dad.

Did you know?

Petoskey stones have been easily found on the shores of Lake Michigan and some inland lakes in Michigan for a very long time. But it wasn't until 1969 that the specific type of coral was identified as *Hexagonaria percarinata* (HEX-A-GUN-AIR-IA PER-CARE-IN-OTA). Yes, this is a super scientific word! While this type of fossilized coral can be found in several places throughout the world, it is most commonly found in Northern Michigan. The best places in Michigan to look for Petoskey stones are near Petoskey, Traverse City, Leelanau County, Harbor Springs, and Charlevoix.

"**C**ome on," I say to my sisters. "Let's go swimming, and afterwards we can look for more Petoskey stones."

And off the three sisters go, splashing and playing in the cool, fresh water on the most perfect hot summer day in Northern Michigan.

Fill your pockets, but not buckets!

You may only collect up to 25 pounds of Petoskey stones per year. But if you are hunting stones along the Sleeping Bear Dunes National Lakeshore, you may look and touch, but not take. Put them back where you found them to preserve nature.

Did you know the best time to look for Petoskey stones is in the spring? This is because the ice and waves shift and move rocks during the winter, bringing them to shore for us to find in the spring.

The Petoskey stone got its name from an Odawa Indian chief, Pet-O-Sega. Pet-O-Sega translates roughly to "rays of sunlight." The town of Petoskey, Michigan, was named in Pet-O-Sega's honor. Descendants of the Odawa tribe still live in the Petoskey area today.

Reference: *Petoskey Stone: Finding, Identifying, and Collecting Michigan's Most Storied Fossil* by Dan R. Lynch

Photography credit: Rolling Fields Photography

Brittany Darga

About the Author

BRITTANY DARGA, a Northern Michigan native, received a bachelor's degree from Western Michigan University and a master's degree from Marquette University. She has worked in the journalism, public relations, and corporate communications fields. Her passion is writing stories and creating curious minds in children.

When she's not writing, her favorite things to do are roam the beach in all seasons, swim, run half marathons, cross-country ski, go on nature walks, read historical fiction, and play with her kids and dog. She lives with her family in Traverse City, Michigan.

More about the author Brittany Darga at

brittanydargaauthor.com

Jennifer Franzoni

About the Illustrator

JENNIFER FRANZONI (Oltersdorf) is a Northern Michigan oil painter, quilter, and mixed media artist. After completing a bachelor of fine arts at Michigan State University, Jennifer settled in Traverse City, Michigan. Her work focuses on large, bold landscapes depicting Leelanau County and the surrounding areas. Everything she creates is built by hand, by her.

Jennifer can be found hiking and exploring during every season of the year, finding new and beloved locations to work from. When she is not working, Jennifer is spending time with her husband, two boys, and dog.

Find her on Instagram:

Jenniferfranzoni.artist

And on her website:

jfranzoniartist.com

Made in the USA
Columbia, SC
14 May 2024

35623946R00020